EXPLORING
CAREERS

Careers in Engineering

Bonnie Szumski

ReferencePoint
Press®

San Diego, CA

© 2015 ReferencePoint Press, Inc.
Printed in the United States

For more information, contact:
ReferencePoint Press, Inc.
PO Box 27779
San Diego, CA 92198
www.ReferencePointPress.com

Picture Credits:
AP Images: 30, 46
Joho Cultura/Newscom: 11
A. Guillotte: 6

LIBRARY OF CONGRESS CATALOGING-IN-PUBLICATION DATA

Szumski, Bonnie, 1958-
  Careers in engineering / by Bonnie Szumski
  Includes bibliographical references and index.
  ISBN-13: 978-1-60152-676-2 (hardback)
  ISBN-10: 1-60152-676-8 (hardback)
  1. Engineering--Vocational guidance--Juvenile literature II. Title.
  TA157.S96 2015
  620.0023--dc23
                                                        2013048093

Contents

A Recession-Proof Profession

Long thought of as the domain of nerds and techies, the field of engineering is becoming increasingly popular and continues to offer some of the most reliable, highly paid professions in the United States. According to Tony Lee, publisher of the online newsletter *CareerCast*, which forecasts career stability, "We're enjoying a true technology revolution, and techies who can lead that effort by creating and managing great software can write their own tickets. Software engineers are the rock stars of today's working world, and even computer systems analysts and web developers can claim some of that recognition, since the demand for IT pros is so deep."

It is not just software engineers who have developed some cachet. In the TV series *Breaking Bad*, a chemistry teacher, clearly well versed in mechanical and chemical engineering, becomes a virtual superman—albeit an evil one—defeating sophisticated drug dealers as well as clever criminals and murderers by using his knowledge of manipulating materials. Environmental disasters such as the 2011 nuclear plant accident in Japan, as well as well-known environmental problems such as global warming, have brought to the fore the need for civil engineers to build and repair and for environmental engineers to help clean up and prevent such trends. Even the war in Afghanistan has highlighted professionals such as biomedical engineers, who design new, sophisticated prosthetic limbs and appliances for those who have lost their limbs in the war.

High-Paying Jobs

Engineers experience some of the lowest unemployment rates of any profession. Even when the economy was at its worst in 2009, while all occupations averaged an unemployment rate of 10 percent, engineers had a much lower 6 percent rate. Within two years, while other occupations were barely recovering, engineers quickly rebounded with an unemployment rate of 2 percent, which has remained steady. The Bureau of Labor Statistics predicts that some areas of engineering will grow far more quickly than other professions in the next fifteen years. These include biomedical, software, and environmental engineering. Environmental engineers, for example, are predicted to experience a 22 percent increase in job opportunities through 2020.

Engineers also enjoy some of the highest starting salaries of any profession. According to the Society for Human Resource Management, starting salaries for engineering students went up 2.3 percent to more than $62,000 in 2013. And while much of the graduating class of 2013 was finding it difficult to land jobs, engineering students were being recruited by technical companies across the nation. In fact, according to a survey conducted by the National Association of Colleges and Employers, six of the ten college majors with the highest starting salaries are in some branch of engineering. Those top majors include computer engineering at $70,400, chemical engineering at $66,400, aerospace/aeronautical/astronautical engineering at $64,000, mechanical engineering at $62,900, electrical/electronics and communications engineering at $62,300, and civil engineering at $57,600. Engineers' salaries do not stop there—they continue to rise, even if engineers do not switch jobs or jump to managerial positions. According to the American Society of Civil Engineers, the median income of full-time salaried engineers regularly increased depending on the amount of time they had been in the job. While the starting salary was $55,000 a year for those with less than one year of experience, those who stayed in the profession for twenty-five years or more earned an average of $127,800 a year. Engineers continue to be compensated more than workers in other fields, in part because they must continually update their knowledge and skills. Many engineers must attend seminars and learn new computer languages and technologies to keep abreast of ongoing changes in their profession.

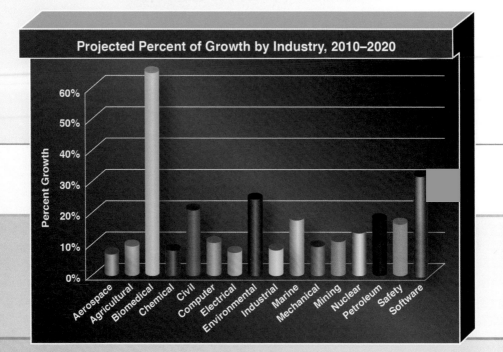

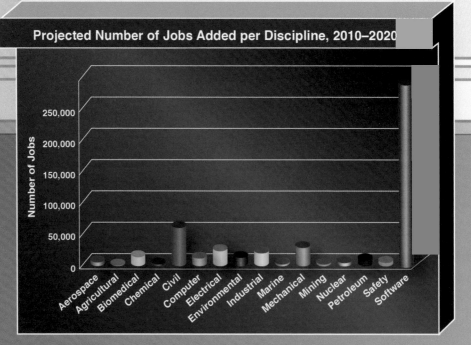

Source: EngineerJobs.com, "Where Will the Engineer Jobs Be in 2020?," November 30, 2012. www.engineerjobs.com.

A Solid Career Choice

Many jobs across the United States are moving overseas because companies believe that outsourcing will allow them to save money. While this trend affects some engineering careers such as electrical engineers who design electronics, many engineering professions must remain in the United States. For example, civil engineers who work on large-scale projects such as freeways, subways, and other urban projects are required to be on-site. Electrical engineers and aerospace engineers often must have high-level security clearance to work on projects for the US military. Such clearance is not granted to overseas producers and requires US citizenship.

Engineering is a solid career because technology is becoming ever more a part of our world. Many technologies—such as computer-based systems, improvements in fuel efficiency and materials of automobiles, new military aircraft and technologies such as drones or the *International Space Station*, new medicines and high-tech materials such as Kevlar, and the newest plastics—are all the purview of the engineer. And this is just a small list of the many ways the engineering professions contribute to life in the modern world. Thomas G. Loughlin, executive director of the American Society of Mechanical Engineers, is quoted in the engineering consulting firm Exact-Source's *PEN* blog as saying: "In November 2011, we surpassed 7 billion people on the planet and it's going to be engineers who create an environment that we can all live on this planet and share resources in an effective and meaningful way." As Loughlin's comment suggests, many engineers believe they are making a difference in people's lives, and they consider their work to be both interesting and meaningful.

Depth and Diversity

Variety is one hallmark of the engineering professions. Engineers in different fields and even in the same fields can find themselves working on a wide array of projects. For instance, one mechanical engineer is working on a refrigerated ice rink that he designed for the National Hockey League. Another works for a company that produces water systems that run on solar power. A software engineer is in charge of keeping a large corporation's computer network system running, as well as adapting software to meet the corporation's needs. An electrical engineer is redesigning military aircraft components. And a chemical engineer is working on the latest biofuels.

Although engineering is one of the most interesting careers, it is not for everyone. All engineers admit that it requires an interest in and a talent for science and math. Dedicated engineers must love to solve problems, remain patient when different avenues do not succeed, and have the perseverance to keep trying. They must also sometimes dedicate long hours and spend most of those hours indoors at a computer. Finally, they must be dedicated to lifelong learning and be good communicators and team players, since the job requires working with many others to make a project come to fruition.

Electrical Engineer

What Does an Electrical Engineer Do?

Electrical engineers work with the production and distribution of electricity. For example, they might work with generators, transmission lines, and transformers. They can design, develop, and make products that generate or use electricity, such as electric motors and ignition systems for automobiles, aircraft, or other engines. They can also design and develop devices such as high-definition televisions, global positioning systems, embedded computer systems, solar power generators, microprocessor chips, robots, and laser systems. Because the field of electrical engineering is so broad, it is often broken into three subsets—analog, digital, and radio frequency. Engineers who specialize in one of these subsets might work in concert or separately on a particular project, such as a device for playing video games. The digital engineer, for example, would be involved in the design of the processors and memory that make up the basic hardware design of the device. The analog engineer would work on the way other hardware such as joysticks, buttons, or instruments interface with the device.

At a Glance:
Electrical Engineer

Minimum Educational Requirements
Bachelor's degree

Personal Qualities
Detail oriented, mechanically inclined, likes science and technical subjects

Certification and Licensing
Voluntary

Working Conditions
Mostly indoors; some travel may be required

Salary Range
About $56,500 to $137,000

Number of Jobs
As of 2013 about 160,560 in the United States

Future Job Outlook
Slower than other categories of engineers; growth rate of 6 percent per year from 2010 to 2020

The analog engineer would also figure out how these ancillary devices would use a shared power supply and how they would interact with the other devices. Finally, a radio frequency engineer would work on any device that had a wireless component. If the game had wireless headphones, for example, or wireless sensors, the radio frequency person would need to figure out how these devices would transmit, send, and interpret a signal from the gaming device.

How Do You Become an Electrical Engineer?

Education

Though it is not necessary to start thinking about an electrical engineering career in high school, many high school students interested in this career take classes in algebra, trigonometry, calculus, biology, physics, chemistry, computer science, and word processing. Electrical engineers typically earn a bachelor of science degree in the subject. Colleges vary in their electrical engineering programs, so it is a good idea to look at several different schools to compare their programs. Some colleges may actually have different degrees in different specialties such as power generation, control systems, communications, or electronics. All engineering students must take courses in mathematical logic and theory, algorithms, numerical methods and analysis, and probability and statistics. They may also take courses in physics and chemistry, computer programming, computer architecture and switching, and mechanics and thermodynamics. Electrical engineering majors learn the physics of electricity and magnetism, the mathematics of circuits and systems, and the engineering tools of analysis and design. Some students go on to earn an additional two-year master of science degree or a four-year PhD in their chosen specialty.

Certification and Licensing

Some electrical engineers may choose to seek one of two levels of licensure. In addition to their degree, professional engineers (PEs) must have four years of work experience and pass a written exam, Principles and Practice of Engineering. Some students pursue another route to the same goal by taking and passing the Fundamentals

An electrical engineer conducts tests in a manufacturing plant. Jobs done by electrical engineers can include working with generators and transmission lines, developing electric motors and ignition systems for automobiles and aircraft, and designing global positioning systems and solar power generators.

of Engineering exam immediately after graduation. Those graduates are then designated as engineers in training or engineer interns. After acquiring work experience, they can take the final exam and gain a full PE certification. Many companies will not hire an engineer unless he or she has attained this certification.

Volunteer Work and Internships

There are many opportunities for students who are interested in preparing for college study of electrical engineering or just finding out if the profession is suitable for them. With the help of a mentor or interested teacher, some high school students choose to engage in an experiment such as building a computer or radio. Some join science clubs like the

Technology Student Association that provide learning opportunities such as design competitions or hands-on projects. Some universities offer science camps and programs to interested high school students.

Opportunities are also available through professional organizations such as the Student Professional Awareness Committee, which works with Institute of Electrical and Electronics Engineers Student Branches in US universities to provide career guidance and promote student awareness of professional issues. Through participation in Student Professional Awareness Conferences, one-day events that students organize and conduct, future electrical engineers hear practicing engineers discuss career issues such as professional ethics, registration, and continuing education. The Student Professional Awareness Venture program offers students the opportunity to design their own professional-awareness activities, with support from the Student Professional Awareness Committee.

Skills and Personality

Electrical engineers need many different skills to be successful. They must be good at math, science, and problem solving. They must enjoy noodling on a problem and trying many different methods to achieve a goal. They must have tenacity and focus. Because this career involves technology that is ever changing, they must also enjoy learning new skills. Other, less scientific skills are also needed, including the ability to write clearly, since an engineer must communicate what he or she has done in written specifications, and to speak clearly, since he or she must often give presentations to explain how and why a particular solution will work. Finally, because electrical engineers must work closely with others, they need to be able to work well as part of a team.

Electrical engineering professor Stewart Personick worked for Bell Laboratories for twenty-eight years before becoming a professor at the New Jersey Institute of Technology in the early 2000s. In an interview on the institute's website, Personick describes some of the characteristics that can be an advantage in electrical engineering:

> Learn to love ambiguity and chaos. Well defined and stable engineering tasks can be easily outsourced. Engineers who can perform such tasks are not in short supply. However,

the definition of what is needed is rapidly evolving: to meet changing customer requirements, changing regulations, and a changing competitive environment, then the task is much harder to outsource. You can make yourself rarer, and thus increase the demand for your talents, by being able to work well with others in a context of rapid change.

On the Job

Employers

The need for electrical engineers has grown exponentially as the world has become more computerized and technology based. According to the Bureau of Labor Statistics, electrical and electronics engineers work primarily in engineering services firms, electric power generation, manufacturing, and research and development. About 22 percent work in companies related to architecture, and 10 percent work with firms producing devices having to do with navigation, measuring, control instruments, and machines that are related to the electro-medical fields. Another 10 percent work in the field of electric power generation, transmission, and distribution; 7 percent work in companies that design or manufacture semiconductors or other electronic components; and 5 percent work in scientific research and development. Commenting on what an electrical engineer might do in the defense industry, Paul Jones, enterprise integration manager at BAE Systems, says on the online career website TARGETJobs:

> At BAE systems—and at most other defense companies—engineers today mainly work at system level. A "system" could be an aircraft or submarine, or one of its major components, or the whole battle space in which it operates, including the associated communications technologies, people, buildings and legal requirements. Defense systems are now so integrated that engineers need to operate cross-discipline, for example using a mixture of mechanical, electronic and electrical engineering knowledge.

Most engineers work full time, and overtime is not uncommon. Potential employers include almost any type of manufacturer of technology items such as computers and cell phones, as well as branches of the military or businesses that are involved in designing weaponry and machinery, automotive electronics, and scientific equipment. They may work for public utilities, private companies, or as freelance consultants.

Working Conditions

For the most part, electrical engineers work indoors in an office, lab, or factory. They often work long hours. As part of their job, some travel to install, repair, or monitor products they have worked on that are installed in different locations.

Earnings

According to the Bureau of Labor Statistics, 160,560 electrical engineers were employed in the United States in 2013. They earned from $56,500 to $137,000 a year, with a median income of $87,920. Some of the highest-paid electrical engineers work in the aerospace industry and make more than $100,000 a year. Other high-paying fields are in electronic component manufacturing and oil and gas extraction. These types of jobs generally pay more than $90,000 a year. The states that employ the most electrical engineers are California and Texas. Most companies offer competitive benefits packages to their employees.

Opportunities for Advancement

Electrical engineers can take additional classes or attend in-house training programs to increase their expertise in particular areas. Those who gain more technical skills or who are good at particular types of work are often offered promotions. More traditional means of gaining promotions, such as becoming a supervisor or taking on positions in sales, are also available. All electrical engineers must continue to learn new skills as technologies change, and those who are adept at learning these skills often advance further than others.

What Is the Future Outlook for Electrical Engineers?

Compared to other types of engineers, jobs for electrical engineers are expected to grow slower than average, with a 6 percent increase from 2010 to 2020. One reason for this, according to the Bureau of Labor Statistics, is that electrical engineers tend to stay in their jobs past the typical retirement age of sixty-two.

While the demand for products and services that electrical engineers work on continues to grow, foreign countries are expected to offer stiff competition in the field. US companies are outsourcing research and design of many products to electrical engineering companies in other countries. This outsourcing is expected to limit the growth of jobs for electrical engineers in the United States. In addition to competition for work with foreign countries, electrical engineers who cannot keep up with changes in technology are subject to layoffs.

However, the global nature of electrical engineering means the availability of international opportunities. According to Blaz Rozer on the website StudyPortals:

> Working as an electrical engineer offers you lots of opportunities in other countries. Laws of math, electricity and physics are universal and your gained knowledge doesn't limit you to only the country you studied in. There are a lot of international companies that need electrical engineers, also most of them are willing to employ people from other countries, and most of them operate on an international level that offers you additional options of traveling while working.

The profession has undergone considerable changes in recent decades, but Personick sees a wide-open future for electrical engineers. He says:

> Current and emerging opportunities that combine electrical engineering with other disciplines include "smart" power grids and "smart" homes, which optimize the use of energy resources, allow alternative energy sources to be used effectively

and encourage energy conservation; applications of new types of patient-monitoring devices, in combination with wireless metropolitan area networks, which provide improved outpatient care and reduce the cost of healthcare; applications of new sensors, in combination with wireless networks to improve indoor air quality and to provide improved safety and security in office buildings and residences; and "smart" highways and associated automated vehicle control systems that can facilitate smooth traffic flows to save time and to reduce pollution and improve highway safety.

Find Out More

American Society for Engineering Education (ASEE)
1818 N St. NW, Suite 600
Washington, DC 20036
phone: (202) 331-3500
fax: (202) 265-8504
website: www.asee.org

The ASEE develops policies and programs that enhance professional opportunities for engineering faculty members and promotes activities that support increased student enrollments in engineering and engineering technology colleges and universities.

Institute of Electrical and Electronics Engineers-USA (IEEE-USA)
2001 L St. NW
Washington, DC 20036
phone: (202) 785-0017
fax: (202) 785-0835
e-mail: ieeeusa@ieee.org
website: www.ieeeusa.org

The IEEE-USA informs and educates IEEE members in the United States about trends, issues, and actions affecting their professional careers. The group prepares positions and recommends appropriate action to public and private decision makers and responds to members' requests for information.

International Electrotechnical Commission (IEC)
Regional Centre for North America
446 Main St., 16th Floor
Worcester, MA 01608
phone: (508) 755-5663
website: www.iec.ch

The IEC is the world's leading organization for the preparation and publication of International Standards for all electrical, electronic, and related technologies, known collectively as electrotechnology. The IEC offers a series of lectures and provides access to a selection of working documents for academic institutions worldwide through its "Academia" section of the website.

Technology Student Association (TSA)
1914 Association Dr.
Reston, VA 20191
phone: (703) 860-9000; toll-free: (888) 860-9010
fax: (703) 758-4852
e-mail: general@tsaweb.org
website: www.tsaweb.org

The TSA fosters personal growth, leadership, and opportunities in technology, innovation, design, and engineering. Members apply and integrate science, technology, engineering, and mathematics concepts through co-curricular activities, competitive events, and related programs.

Civil Engineer

What Does a Civil Engineer Do?

Civil engineers are responsible for designing the infrastructure that people interact with every day. They represent arguably one of the oldest professions, because humans have been driven to build structures since the beginnings of civilization. Civil engineers design and supervise the construction of roads, buildings, airports, tunnels, dams, bridges, and sewage and treatment plants. Civil engineers work on the problems of everyday life—what people are most likely to need, how they will access it, and how to build and maintain it.

There is a lot of variety in this profession, because human infrastructure is vast and complicated. Freeway construction projects provide a good example. Civil engineers may begin with designing the freeway in a software program to see the most effective location and layout of the freeway. Civil engineers called geotechnical engineers analyze reports having to do with the soil structure and whether it can withstand such a project. For freeways designed with buildings and tunnels, geotechnical engi-

---

At a Glance:

Civil Engineer

Minimum Educational Requirements
Bachelor's degree

Personal Qualities
Detail oriented, mechanically inclined, likes science and technical subjects; mastery of written and oral communication

Certification and Licensing
Voluntary

Working Conditions
Mostly indoors; some travel may be required

Salary Range
About $50,000 to $119,000

Number of Jobs
As of 2013 about 240,000 in the United States

Future Job Outlook
Growth rate of 19 percent from 2010 to 2020

---

neers figure out how such structures interact with the soil and rock and recommend changes if they determine that additional support is needed. Civil engineers also suggest and design slopes, retaining walls, and other structures to help, for example, with weather extremes in the area. They also evaluate how rain runoff will affect local communities around the freeway and plan for ways to help handle the runoff. Sometimes special considerations are needed for areas with particularly unstable soil. For example, on the Qinghai Railroad in Tibet, engineers had to figure out how to build across the permafrost, a thin layer of frozen soil that is highly susceptible to temperature variation. They decided to build a large section of the railway aboveground, with the track balanced on posts that were buried deep in the mud under the permafrost. Solving these types of problems is a large part of a civil engineer's job.

One type of civil engineer, known as a structural engineer, is involved in planning bridges, tunnels, and dams. This type of civil engineer determines which combination of materials would be best for the structure; how much concrete, asphalt, and steel would be required to build it; and how much the materials and labor would cost.

Another type of civil engineer is a transportation engineer. Transportation engineers analyze data having to do with traffic statistics, where and how people access roads, and potential obstacles and traffic jams. They analyze the cost of building new transportation structures and analyze the environmental factors that would need to be considered during construction.

All civil engineers must be knowledgeable about environmental considerations and restrictions in particular areas. For example, in earthquake-prone areas such as California, civil engineers must understand the state's regulations regarding new construction and take into account what type of building materials are needed to meet the state standards. If structures are to be built near water or vulnerable groundwater supplies, civil engineers must conform to federal standards regarding environmental protections.

After deciding on the parameters of any large-scale public project, civil engineers present their findings to the public and/or the government for approval. Because many large-scale projects are under tight deadlines and strict cost controls, civil engineers must be good at projecting project completion time and be adept at budget projections.

People who become civil engineers tend to receive a lot of satisfaction from their jobs because they can say, "I helped build that." Their contribution to society is the most recognizable, as everyone can appreciate a well-built road, tunnel, or building. Civil engineers are also admired when they build a structure that takes into account particular challenges of an area and overcome seemingly amazing challenges, such as with the section of the BART transportation system that operates underwater in the San Francisco Bay. Rebecca Clark is a civil engineer and project manager at Skanska Koch, a division of the construction/engineering giant Skanska USA that specializes in building infrastructure such as roads, bridges, and tunnels. In an interview on the website EngineeringJobs.com, she agrees that building something is the most exciting part of her career: "The best part of the job is the ability to make a tangible difference. No matter which way you look at it, being involved in the infrastructure and components involved in transportation makes a big difference. It is a lifeline for a city, for people. You can physically see what you've built. And the revisions you've made."

How Do You Become a Civil Engineer?

Education

All civil engineers have at least a bachelor's degree. As with other careers that require a college education, it is wise to take classes in high school to prepare for college. For civil engineering, students need to take higher mathematics classes such as algebra, trigonometry, and calculus, as well as classes in science such as physics, chemistry, and computer science.

Because civil engineering is so varied, many students choose a specialty as an undergraduate, including structural analysis, materials design, geology, hydraulics, surveying, soil mechanics, or oceanography. Although it is not required, about 30 percent of students go on to attain a master's degree in a chosen specialty. Students should ensure that the civil engineering program at their college of choice has been approved by ABET (formerly the Accreditation Board for Engineering and Technology). A program accredited by ABET is needed in order to gain licensure, which is required to work as a PE.

Certification and Licensing

Civil engineers who want to work on public works must attain a PE license. Such a license is required by all fifty states and Washington, DC. States require licensure because the government sponsors many large-scale engineering projects, which carry with them a large amount of liability for people's lives.

Volunteer Work and Internships

There are many opportunities for students who are interested to prepare for a college career in civil engineering or find out if the profession is suitable for them. Along with a mentor or interested teacher, some high school students choose to join science clubs like the Technology Student Association that provide learning opportunities such as design competitions or hands-on projects. Other universities offer science camps and programs to interested high school students. Some civil engineers suggest volunteering on or getting a job in construction or a road crew to gain firsthand knowledge about how civil engineers manage large-scale projects and solve problems on the job.

Engineering societies such as the American Society of Civil Engineers (ASCE) offers opportunities such as conferences, awards, and career help for students who are interested in or majoring in civil engineering. ASCE Student Conferences are held every spring in locations around the country. Most of these conferences include a business meeting, professional/technical presentations, competitions (surveying, technical paper presentations, building projects such as a concrete canoe, or a steel bridge), social activities, and an awards banquet.

Skills and Personality

Civil engineering requires an interest in the sciences and mathematics. It also requires a passion for problem solving and a facile mind that is willing to look at a problem from many different angles. In addition, civil engineers require good interpersonal skills because they are often called upon to work in a team and good communication skills because they must often write down the specifications for a project and communicate their ideas to others. Clark commented on why she became a civil engineer:

> I loved math and always, always had a passion for bridges. Really, I've always been awed by bridges. And I think one of my grandfathers once told me, "I think you should be an engineer." So since the 7th or 8th grade I've always talked about being an engineer and I think that really set the course. That was all I wanted to be.
>
> And for me, becoming an engineer was an important way to tangibly make a difference in the lives of others. The infrastructure of a city is its blood and lifeline. Buildings and sewage and bridges and tunnels and water—all are affiliated with infrastructure. Understanding how they are all connected is the equivalent of understanding how a city (and an economy) works. Infrastructure equals the heartbeat and pulse of a city.

On the Job

Employers

There are many career paths within this field. Specialties include architectural, structural, transportation, traffic, water resources, and geotechnical engineering. Civil engineers may work for state or local governments or in the private sector at consulting or construction firms. Some civil engineers go into supervisory or administrative positions, and others pursue careers in design, construction, or teaching. The largest employers of engineers, at around 48 percent, are in the architectural and related fields. State governments employ 13 percent of the civil engineers, local governments employ 11 percent, and the federal government employs the smallest number, at around 5 percent. Another 5 percent work in nonresidential construction.

Civil engineering is one of the engineering careers that attracts women, and many women report that, though they have a tough time competing with men for promotions and pay, they are finding more acceptance in this career. In an interview on the Engineer Girl website, president and chief executive officer of Pegasus Global Holdings Patricia Galloway explained:

> Large contractors these days are actively seeking young women engineers whom they can employ, teach, and move into their management positions. It is not just about gender diversity, but the fact that women offer and contribute to the team from different perspectives, thus making the team stronger and better posed to completing the project on time and on budget. Owners, too, are employing more and more women engineers and those designing and constructing projects are also actively involving their women engineers in the field. I have been in the construction industry for 32 years and LOVE IT!! . . . But be sure to always learn. Continuing education and certification is very important to your career and you want to continue to do this as well as volunteer for leadership positions within your local professional societies.

Working Conditions

Civil engineers work mostly indoors but must travel to solve problems or answer questions on-site. Many engineers travel internationally to work on large projects in other countries. They also must be prepared to devote a lot of time and attention to their jobs. "There are times you have to be on site in the middle of the night because there's an emergency. Your job is around the clock," says Clark. "And, also, it's a dangerous job. You are, on occasion, exposed to fatalities on the job. There is a lot of liability in construction and as a project manager you are responsible for people's safety. Everyone preaches safety but ensuring it is different. And when your job involves people's lives it takes it up a few notches."

Earnings

The highest-paid civil engineers work on, maintain, and repair commercial and industrial equipment. The areas with the highest-paid engineers are in Louisiana and Southern and central California.

Opportunities for Advancement

In large firms, civil engineers follow a career path of moving from junior engineer, through assistant engineer, to associate engineer, to project management. In smaller companies, civil engineers usually form a specialization and are paid more for that area of expertise. Civil engineers can also form their own firm and contract out particular aspects of large public works jobs, for example.

What Is the Future Outlook for Civil Engineers?

Civil engineers are expected to outpace their counterparts in other engineering fields. Whereas other engineering sectors are expected to grow by 10 percent, civil engineering is expected to grow by 19 percent. This is largely due to an older and deteriorating infrastructure in the United States. Sewage and water lines in many states are very old and in need of rebuilding. Aging roadways and bridges are also expected to need redesign and refurbishing. In addition, the worldwide population is expected to grow exponentially, and US engineers are expected to fill many positions as American companies gain jobs in other countries. Areas of special interest include building water- and sewage-delivery systems as well as planning roads and freeways in underdeveloped or emerging nations.

Find Out More

American Society for Engineering Education (ASEE)
1818 N St. NW, Suite 600
Washington, DC 20036
phone: (202) 331-3500
fax: (202) 265-8504
website: www.asee.org

The ASEE develops policies and programs that enhance professional opportunities for engineering faculty members and promotes activities that support increased student enrollments in engineering and engineering technology colleges and universities. The ASEE also fulfills its mission by providing a valuable communication link among corporations, government agencies, and educational institutions.

American Society of Civil Engineers (ASCE)
1801 Alexander Bell Dr.
Reston, VA 20191
phone: (800) 548-2723
website: www.asce.org

The ASCE represents more than 140,000 members of the civil engineering profession worldwide and is America's oldest national engineering society. The society seeks to advance the profession of civil engineering and serve the public good.

Institute of Transportation Engineers (ITE)
1627 Eye St. NW, Suite 600
Washington, DC 20006
phone: (202) 785-0060
e-mail: ite_staff@ite.org
website: www.ite.org

The ITE is an international educational and scientific association of transportation professionals who are responsible for meeting mobility and safety needs. Through its products and services, the ITE promotes professional development of its members, supports and encourages education, stimulates research, develops public awareness programs, and serves as a conduit for the exchange of professional information.

Technology Student Association (TSA)
1914 Association Dr.
Reston, VA 20191
phone: (703) 860-9000; toll-free: (888) 860-9010
fax: (703) 758-4852
e-mail: general@tsaweb.org
website: www.tsaweb.org

The TSA fosters personal growth, leadership, and opportunities in technology, innovation, design, and engineering. Members apply and integrate science, technology, engineering, and mathematics concepts through co-curricular activities, competitive events, and related programs.

Biomedical Engineer

What Does a Biomedical Engineer Do?

Biomedical engineering is a relatively new field, and much of the work these engineers do is cutting-edge. Biomedical engineers have been involved in the mapping of the human genome; the development of robotics; the engineering of body tissues, including artificial organs; and nanotechnology. They are responsible for finding ways to make adult stem cells function like fetal stem cells. They have developed advanced artificial limbs that respond to signals from the brain. They are responsible for the treatment of many diseases, including brain implants that help Parkinson's patients communicate and calm tremors. They have even been involved in agriculture and the design of genetically engineered crops. In the broadest sense, biomedical engineers solve problems related to biology and medicine. They may design instruments, devices, and software or conduct research or design ways to test new drugs or medical devices. They also design reha-

At a Glance:

Biomedical Engineer

Minimum Educational Requirements
Bachelor's degree

Personal Qualities
Must have an excellent grasp of and enjoy the sciences, math, and chemistry; enjoy learning and problem solving

Certification and Licensing
Voluntary

Working Conditions
Indoors

Salary Range
About $59,000 to $126,990

Number of Jobs
As of 2013 about 15,700 in the United States

Future Job Outlook
Much better than average; growth rate of 62 percent from 2010 to 2020

bilitative exercise equipment. To perform their job, biomedical engineers must understand human biology and technology.

These engineers often must combine areas of expertise in their daily work. For example, designing computer software to run complicated medical instruments requires programming knowledge as well as an understanding of the mechanics behind medical devices. Likewise, engineers who work on drug therapies must have knowledge of chemistry and biology. They usually work as part of a team that includes people with medical expertise in the field they are working in.

The profession of biomedical engineering has many specialties:

- Bioinstrumentation engineers work on devices that diagnose and treat disease. In this arena, knowledge of computers is essential.
- Biomaterials engineers design, test, and research materials that will be used in the replacement of living tissue and implants. They must test these materials for safety, endurance, and strength. They must also make sure that these materials will not cause an adverse reaction in the body.
- Biomechanics engineers use their knowledge of mechanics and apply that knowledge to the body to better understand how these areas intersect and how they can be used together to improve quality of life. Biomechanical engineers sometimes work on products and treatments related to one particular part of the body, such as the cardiovascular system.
- Cellular, tissue, and genetics engineers work at the cellular level to understand how diseases attack the cells and how to intervene to help those cells fight off disease.
- Clinical engineers are hired by hospitals to help purchase medical instruments and adapt those instruments to respond to the needs of physicians and the hospital. They must understand and maintain advanced medical machinery and have knowledge of computer instrumentation.
- Medical imaging engineers develop diagnostic equipment that produces images that doctors can interpret and understand in order to treat patients. They must understand the principles of sound, radiation, and magnetism.

- Orthopedic engineers design artificial joints and study the way joints move.
- Rehabilitation engineers design and develop artificial limbs and rehabilitative equipment.
- Systems physiology engineers develop and design computer models to analyze data related to the way living organisms function. They work at the microscopic level and may study skin and how it heals itself or responds to a particular drug.

Lori Laird is a biomedical engineer who designs noninvasive instruments and tools for use by vascular surgeons in the treatment of blocked arteries. She also works with manufacturing personnel on issues of design for manufacturing and quality control. When asked what her typical day was like on the website TryEngineering, Laird replied:

> Yesterday was a good day. I did a lot of different things yesterday. I started out with a meeting. Actually, I started out checking out e-mail and voice mail and writing myself my "to do" list for today; these are the things I'm going to accomplish. I went to a meeting in the morning. After that, I went to a class where they teach about the safety of blood-borne pathogens. In medical devices, there are a lot of safety and medical issues. We handle devices as they come back from the field to check them out for defects and things like that. And I took a class on how to handle the devices and not get contaminated by the blood. After that, I checked out one of the tools. We're having a problem with one of our tools on the manufacturing line. So I sat down, I called the vendor and talked to them about different ways to make this tool. Did a little bit of designing.

How Do You Become a Biomedical Engineer?

Education

High school students interested in a biomedical engineering career need to take science, chemistry, physics, and biology courses. In addition, courses in higher mathematics such as algebra and calculus are good options. Those students interested in the design part of this discipline would benefit from drafting, mechanical drawing, or computer programming courses as well.

Students who pursue this major in college need to find a degree program that is accredited by ABET. Degree programs focus on engineering coupled with the biological sciences—such as physiology, pharmacology, and biology. These courses also require hours in a laboratory. Other courses that may be included are fluid and solid mechanics, computer programming, circuit design, and biomaterials.

Many students go on to pursue postgraduate education in a particular field of bioengineering. These students often learn more practical application of their education by working with a faculty member on a project or research experiment.

Certification and Licensing

As with other engineering careers, certification is required if the engineer is planning on working on projects that affect the health, safety, or life of the public. They must attain a PE license. Such a license is required by all fifty states and Washington, DC.

Volunteer Work and Internships

High school students interested in this career should apply for internships at hospitals. In addition, participating in science fairs is good way to learn about developing products or designing research. Undergraduate students in accredited programs are offered many opportunities for volunteer programs, many of which include internships at hospitals.

Skills and Personality

A love of continual education is a good quality for a biomedical engineer. Since the career is in constant flux as new technologies are developed, biomedical engineers must learn new techniques and systems. Biomedical engineers must be able to analyze the needs of patients and customers to design appropriate solutions. Although all engineers require good analytical, math, science, and communication skills as well as a love of problem solving, biomedical engineers must

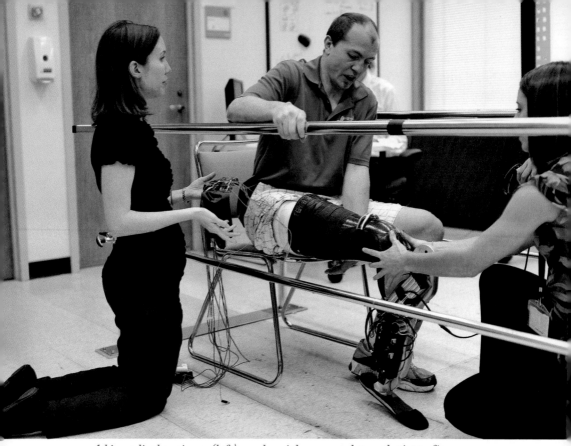

A biomedical engineer (left) works with a research prosthetist to fit an experimental prosthetic leg on a man who lost his leg in a motorcycle accident. In the relatively new field of biomedical engineering, much of the work involves cutting-edge technology and research.

have other qualities as well. Because they work on diverse teams that may include patients, therapists, physicians, and businesspeople, biomedical engineers must have good listening skills to address the needs of these various stakeholders. In addition, biomedical engineers work with biological systems, so they need to be adept both at mechanical applications and the science of the human body.

Laird describes how she got into the biomedical field. She started out as a mechanical engineer.

> I grew up in Los Angeles, Southern California. Started going to school at Long Beach State. And at the time, I still didn't know I wanted to be a mechanical engineer. I tried zoology, because I liked animals. I tried architecture. And then I still wasn't satisfied. And so I took an aptitude test

from the career center at Long Beach State, and they said, "By golly, you should be an engineer." And I always kind of thought in the back of my head that that's what I wanted to do. But I just needed somebody to tell me. And I decided to do mechanical engineering because I've always enjoyed taking things apart. Solving puzzles, solving problems. I enjoy picturing things spatially and in 3D and things like that. And that really drove me down the path of mechanical engineering.

Laird always wanted to be in the biomedical engineering field, but her school did not offer a program specifically in that, so she had to find a way to do it: "I did an emphasis on biomedical. I took more design classes. I took extra biology classes, physiology. . . . I kind of had to create my own degree. And I did senior projects in that area. Did design projects involving biomedical or prosthetics and things like that."

On the Job

Employers

About 15,700 biomedical engineers work in the United States. According to the Bureau of Labor Statistics, most biological engineers—23 percent—work in the medical equipment and manufacturing sector. Scientific research and development makes up 19 percent of the biomedical engineering jobs in the United States, and pharmaceutical and medicine manufacturing make up 14 percent. Academia makes up another 11 percent, with biomedical engineers working at colleges, universities, and professional schools. State, local, and private government jobs make up 11 percent, and general medical and surgical hospitals hold 7 percent.

Biomedical engineers work in many different settings, and much depends on which specialty they are in. Some work in hospitals where therapy occurs, and others work in laboratories doing research. Those with design skills may work in manufacturing.

Working Conditions

Though biomedical engineers mostly work inside in one location, some are required to travel. Biomedical engineers who work with medical machinery such as imaging machinery or with products that affect patients, such as prosthetics, may be required to work on-site testing the new equipment or working with patients who receive the prosthetic devices. They often team up with other professionals when they work directly with patients. As with many other engineering professions, biomedical engineers spend a lot of time working on a single problem. Mark Pagel has been a professor of biomedical engineering at the University of Arizona since 2008. On the website Colleges & Degrees, he explains the importance of being both persistent and patient: "Perseverance is critical in all fields of science and engineering. Research is difficult and many small techniques need to be successful for an entire research experiment to be successful. There is simply no substitute to trying again and again until the experiment is successful. Thomas Edison's perseverance in creating the light bulb is perhaps the best example." He also remarks that writing is important to the profession: "Technical writing is also critical. Biomedical engineers who have the personality traits to communicate their research, and to refine their skills in writing and oral presentations, have a clear advantage."

Earnings

The median annual wage of biomedical engineers was $81,540 in 2010, according to the Bureau of Labor Statistics. The top 10 percent in the profession earned more than $126,990. Because of the many specialties involved, biomedical engineer salaries vary depending on which sector they work in. According to the Bureau of Labor Statistics, wages are as follows: scientific research and development services, $88,330; pharmaceutical and medicine manufacturing, $82,820; medical equipment and supplies manufacturing, $81,150; Colleges, universities, and professional schools—state, local, and private, $68,070; general medical and surgical hospitals—state, local, and private, $59,010.

Opportunities for Advancement

Many biological engineers go on to earn postgraduate degrees in medicine or other specialties. Salaries are tied to these advanced degrees—the more education an engineer has attained, the higher his or her pay.

What Is the Future Outlook for Biomedical Engineers?

The outlook is very good for biomedical engineers. The Bureau of Labor Statistics expects this field to grow by 62 percent from 2010 to 2020, much more quickly than other engineering professions. However, because the field is more specialized, the number of jobs in this field is small to begin with. So even though it is a growing field, there will still be a small total number of jobs.

Increase in demand is tied to the aging baby boom generation, who will require more prosthetics and implants as they age. In addition, new medical advances are continually being researched and designed, further enhancing the need for such engineers.

Find Out More

American Institute for Medical and Biological Engineering (AIMBE)
1701 K St. NW, Suite 510
Washington, DC 20006
phone: (202) 496-9660
website: www.aimbe.org

The AIMBE is a nonprofit organization headquartered in Washington, DC. It represents fifty thousand individuals and the top 2 percent of medical and biological engineers. In addition, the AIMBE represents academic institutions, private industry, and professional engineering societies.

American Society of Agricultural and Biological Engineers (ASABE)
2950 Niles Rd.
St. Joseph, MI 49085
phone: (800) 371-2723

fax: (269) 429-3852
e-mail: hq@asabe.org
website: www.asabe.org

The ASABE has been the professional home of engineers and others worldwide who endeavor to find sustainable solutions for an ever-growing population. This member-driven technical and educational organization provides networking, publications, and student scholarships and awards.

Biomedical Engineering Society (BMES)
8201 Corporate Dr., Suite 1125
Landover, MD 20785
phone: (301) 459-1999; toll-free: (877) 871-2637
fax: (301) 459-2444
website: www.bmes.org

The goal of the BMES is to serve as the world's leading society of professionals devoted to developing and using engineering and technology to advance human health and well-being. The BMES also supports student chapters through the United States. It has a commitment to student learning and posts several educational videos on its website.

National Institute of Biomedical Imaging and Bioengineering (NIBIB)
National Institute of Health
9000 Rockville Pike
Bethesda, MD 20892
phone: (301) 496-4000
website: www.nih.gov

The mission of the NIBIB is to improve health by leading the development and accelerating the application of biomedical technologies. The institute is committed to integrating the physical and engineering sciences with the life sciences to advance basic research and medical care. It offers grants and educational opportunities to those in the field.

Society for Biological Engineers (SBE)
120 Wall St., 23rd Floor
New York, NY 10005-4020
phone: (800) 242-4363
website: www.aiche.org

The SBE is a global organization of leading engineers and scientists dedicated to advancing the integration of biology with engineering. The SBE promotes the integration of biology with engineering and realizes its benefits through bioprocessing, biomedical, and biomolecular applications.

Software Engineer

Software engineers can be involved in the design and development of many types of software for many different businesses. They may work on computer games, business applications, operating systems, and networks. They can also change and convert existing programs to meet the needs of their clients.

At a Glance:
Software Engineer

Minimum Educational Requirements
Bachelor's degree

Personal Qualities
Must enjoy technical and scientific subjects; have perseverance, patience, and passion for accuracy

Certification and Licensing
Voluntary

Working Conditions
Indoors

Salary Range
About $54,840 to $132,080

Number of Jobs
As of 2013 about 494,460 in the United States

Future Job Outlook
A growth rate of 30 percent from 2010 to 2020

Computer software engineers begin by analyzing users' needs and then design, test, and develop software to meet those needs. During this process they create the detailed sets of instructions, called algorithms, that tell the computer what to do. They may convert these instructions into a computer language, but this piece is normally taken over by a computer programmer. Software engineers must be extremely knowledgeable about operating systems. They must also understand middleware, which is the software layer that lies between the operating system and the applications the engineer works on.

Systems software engineers may work on an organization's computer systems software to help it better meet the needs of the staff. They work with every level of the company—including order and fulfillment, inventory, billing, and payroll—to analyze what each stratum of the company needs from the computer system. They also might set up the organization's networks, or intranet, that link computers within the organization and improve communication between departments. These engineers also work on a company's in-house website and external communications.

Systems software engineers also work for companies that configure, implement, and install the computer systems of other organizations. Often they are members of marketing and sales or technical support. Once their company sells a system, the company sends these engineers to work with the purchasers to customize the product to meet customers' needs.

On the website iSEEK, Jim Amweg, a software/firmware engineer for Silent Power in Baxter, Minnesota, describes a typical day:

> My duties include designing, implementing, and testing embedded code that operates our OnDemand energy appliance. . . . My typical day can be summed up in one word: hectic! I typically work anywhere from eight to 14 hours per day designing, coding, answering questions, and providing guidance on an as-needed basis. I have trained some engineering technicians to download the firmware to the processors and do some system-level testing so that my time isn't all eaten up doing that type of job. We really spend very little time in meetings, since there are so few of us trying to do so much, so quickly.

How Do You Become a Software Engineer?

Education

Most software engineers have a bachelor's degree. Some jobs may require only an associate's degree, but others require a master's degree. Software engineers must take courses in computer science, computer information systems, software engineering, or mathematics. Some students take programming and software engineering classes to supplement a degree in another field such as accounting, business, or finance.

Not all software engineers follow this traditional route to a job in the field. Tom Janofsky is vice president of software engineering at Monetate, a Philadelphia-based company. In the May 14, 2012, issue of *Information Week*, he said, "Some people who come to our company and interview for a position may not have even studied to become a software engineer, but maybe wrote a game that's available in an app store. It's very much a field that's open and accessible to people that may not have a traditional computer science background."

Certification and Licensing

Certifications are often offered by software companies who wish to train engineers on particular products. These courses are usually rigorous and may be required by some employers who use a particular type of software.

Volunteer Work and Internships

For college students, hundreds of internships are available to those seeking a software engineering degree. Most internships train students in a particular kind of application, so students should make sure such training matches their career goals. It is not unusual for a company to offer a student intern a job upon graduation.

Skills and Personality

Software engineers must have strong problem-solving and communication skills and an aptitude for math and science. They need to learn and retain computer languages, have attention to detail, and be able to multitask. Software engineers spend long periods sitting at a computer, so those who choose this profession need to enjoy an indoor office environment. They must also have a passion for writing accurate code and have the patience to wait to see the results of their code and redo or fine-tune it. Amweg echoes this description when he says: "Above all, you've got to love writing and debugging code. I tell everyone/anyone who'll listen that it's a good thing I can get paid for doing what I do since I'd be doing it anyhow. I can truthfully say that there is nothing I would rather do than write code to solve a problem."

On the website Wasted Talent, one software engineer describes the characteristics that best serve people in this career:

> Most engineers that I know are a curious sort. When an engineer sees a problem, the first instinct is to think of a solution for it. If the problem is particularly annoying and the solution is within their capabilities, it'll take a lot to convince the engineer in question not to implement the solution. It's also worth noting that most engineers I know can get annoyed at things that are not working as smooth/well as they think it could.

> A particular trait I encounter in my specific field is nerdiness/ geekiness. Being a software engineer, that's sort of a given. In-jokes and quotes run rampant in the office. There's about a 50/50 split between gamers and non-gamers, but I'm guessing that's higher than in most other professions.

Employers

Almost every area of business has a computer dimension. People increasingly use computers to work, shop, entertain, and integrate work and home lives. As demand for products increases, the demand for software engineers and developers will also increase. Just one example is the way that large computer companies are attempting to make software available on tablets. As consumers show their preference for tablets over traditional personal computers, a demand for software to be available for both has increased. Software engineers would definitely be in the front lines of reconfiguring software design for this purpose. Computer software engineers are needed to develop Internet, intranet, and World Wide Web applications. In addition, areas such as data-processing systems in business, telecommunications, government, and other settings add to this ever-expanding field.

The tremendous growth of the Internet, widespread use of websites, and wireless technology has created a need for software that works across platforms such as computers, tablets, and phones. As such demand increases, there will be a need for increased security to prevent the hacking of such devices. This is another growing area of need for software engineers.

And it is not just the consumer market that will need software engineers. The military and other industries will require constant reconfiguring and redesigning of their computer systems as they become more mechanized. The Bureau of Labor Statistics reports that 32 percent of software engineers work in computer systems design and related services; 10 percent in computer and electronic manufacturing; 8 percent in finance and insurance; and 7 percent in the software publishing industry.

Some software engineers are employed on a temporary or contract basis as consultants. Consultants can be brought in to maintain companies' websites and computers or establish entire systems. This segment of the software engineering population is expected to continue to grow as more businesses find that they do not need a full-time staff person but still need ongoing maintenance and repair of their computer systems.

Working Conditions

Software engineers work mainly indoors, usually in a casual environment. They often work in teams that contain people with different expertise. A typical team includes marketing, manufacturing, and design. An increasing number of software engineers are self-employed contractors who are hired on a temporary basis to solve problems or ongoing maintenance issues.

Software engineering is also a good field for women—many are already in the field. Thomson Reuters software engineer Sameena Shah was interviewed on the Engineer Girl website about women in the profession. She says:

The work environment in software companies is thoroughly professional. . . . I would say that nowadays software companies are the best place for women to work in. One is not required to run around, you can work from the comfort of an office or even your own home, and several companies offer flexible hours policy. . . . The lack of women in senior positions has put pressure on senior management to promote better sex ratio for top positions; this makes it easier for motivated women to get promoted quickly.

Earnings

According to the Bureau of Labor Statistics, the salary range for software engineers is $54,840 for an entry-level position to $132,080 for a senior technician. In 2013 the job-search website Indeed listed the average income for a software engineer at $91,000. The salary for a computer software engineer is 111 percent higher than the average salary in the United States and was considered the best job of 2012. Companies that pay software engineers the most include Google, Cisco Systems, Facebook, Apple, and Zynga. Salaries are the highest in cities such as San Francisco, New York, and Chicago. And it looks like these high salaries are going to continue to increase. In the 2012 *Information Week* article, Janofsky comments on rising pay in this field: "Over the last few years there's definitely been a 20% to 25% uptick in salary for software engineers. . . . I feel like I live in a different economy. We're constantly hiring, which is so different from what I hear on the news. It's sort of surreal."

Opportunities for Advancement

Software engineers are typically promoted within three to five years. The typical career track of a software engineer is from entry level to a senior software engineer position. Depending on the company, this position could mean many different things. Two of the most common job titles are software architect, which involves designing software applications and programs, and project management, which involves working on specific large-scale projects. Another advancement opportunity for talented individuals with both computer skills and team-building skills is that of software manager, which involves managing a team of individuals to lead and accomplish a major software project.

What Is the Future Outlook for Software Engineers?

The future outlook for software engineers is better than average, with an expected 30 percent growth in jobs from 2010 to 2020. The unemployment rate for software engineers is extremely low, at 1 percent. The highest demand will be for software engineers who have mastered the most up-to-date programming tools and languages. Opportunities will continue to grow with the advance of mobile phone technology and operating systems, as well as in the health-care industry. Amweg finds one of the most interesting parts of his job to be the way it continues to change: "My only regret is that I wasn't born a little later. The future's going to be very exciting, and I'd really like to be around to see more of it."

Find Out More

Association for Computer Machinery (ACM)
2 Penn Pl., Suite 701
New York, NY 10121
phone: (800) 342-6626
website: www.acm.org

The ACM is the world's largest educational and scientific computing society. It delivers resources that advance computing as a science and a profession. The ACM provides the computing field's premier Digital Library and serves its members and the computing profession with leading-edge publications, conferences, and career resources. For students, the ACM has many resources, including scholarship opportunities.

Association for Women in Computing (AWC)
PO Box 2768
Oakland, CA 94602
e-mail: Info@awc-hq.org

The AWC is one of the first professional organizations for women in computing. The association is dedicated to promoting the advancement of women in the computing professions. The AWC provides opportunities for professional growth through networking and through programs on technical and career-oriented topics.

Association of Software Professionals (ASP)
PO Box 1522
Martinsville, IN 46151
phone: (765) 349-4740
website: www.asp-software.org

The ASP is a professional trade association of more than one thousand software developers who create and market leading-edge applications. Members share their experiences of mastering the most promising technologies, benefiting from new marketing strategies, and working through business challenges.

Institute of Electrical and Electronics Engineers-USA (IEEE-USA)
2001 L St. NW
Washington, DC 20036
phone: (202) 785-0017
fax: (202)785-0835
e-mail: ieeeusa@ieee.org
website: www.ieeeusa.org

The IEEE-USA informs and educates IEEE members in the United States about trends, issues, and actions affecting their professional careers. The Student Professional Awareness Committee works with IEEE Student Branches in US universities to provide career guidance and promote student awareness of professional issues. The Student Professional Awareness Venture program offers students the opportunity to design their own professional-awareness activities, with support from the Student Professional Awareness Committee.

Mechanical Engineer

What Does a Mechanical Engineer Do?

A mechanical engineer is the jack-of-all-trades of the engineering world. As with all engineering professions, the mechanical engineer's strength is solving problems. The job can encompass all phases of development of a new product, from conception, design, implementation, testing, and marketing, to maintenance and redesign.

Mechanical engineers work on a hugely diverse array of projects. In the power-generation world, this engineer can work on electrical generators, internal combustion engines, and steam and gas turbines. Refrigeration and air cooling, robotics, elevators, escalators, and tools are just a few of the additional products mechanical engineers might be involved in. In the forefront of technology, mechanical engineers work on projects involving energy conservation such as solar and water power. Their specialty is how energy is generated, stored, and how it moves. These engineers may work in the gas and oil industry or with alternative energy suppliers. They may work to develop more fuel-efficient cars,

At a Glance:
Mechanical Engineer

Minimum Educational Requirements
Bachelor's degree

Personal Qualities
Detail oriented, mechanically inclined, likes science and technical subjects, problem solver

Certification and Licensing
Voluntary

Working Conditions
Mostly indoors; some travel may be required

Salary Range
About $52,030 to $121,530

Number of Jobs
As of 2013 about 252,540 in the United States

Future Job Outlook
Slower than other categories of engineers; a growth rate of 9 percent from 2010 to 2020

motors, and other machinery. They are also the translators between complex machinery and human users, training technicians who work with their products and reinterpreting and fixing them to work more easily and efficiently for the end users.

Typically, mechanical engineers specialize in one part of the development process. Those who specialize in research look at a given problem from many different angles; they might study existing devices to gain insight into what such devices can already do, and then they might develop a prototype device for testing. From there, a mechanical engineer who specializes in design will try to take the prototype and improve on it, answering the questions of how to make it more streamlined for commercial production and how to produce it efficiently and cost-effectively. A testing engineer then works with the designer to test the product in real-life situations and gather data on the device. He or she will make suggestions on changes and possible improvements. A mechanical engineer who specializes in manufacturing will then make the computations to estimate how to make the device commercially. This can include making a determination about the type and quantity of material needed, which machines to use, how much space is needed to make the product, the total estimated costs, and how much time it will take to bring the product to market. This specialty will also bring in other engineers when needed to advise on aspects of the product. Maintenance and operations specialists work with ongoing issues with the new equipment that makes the product. Sales engineers are responsible for selling and explaining the product to customers. Other mechanical engineers work on products.

Doug Lucht works as a mechanical engineer for Sebesta Blomberg & Associates, a heating and air-conditioning company in Minnesota. In an interview on the website iSEEK, he talks about a typical day:

> I usually start my workday around 8 to 8:30 a.m. My daily work can involve calculations to determine heating and cooling loads or the energy requirements for a building. Often, I am working with a vendor that sells a product we use and am talking about options, limitations, and how their product will work in my project. The work involves attending construction

meetings, going to the project site, reviewing the construction and installation of our systems, meeting with building owners, and more. The day can involve any number of those things, plus internal meetings where we talk about our projects and current assignments. There's a lot of communication happening and a lot of meetings. Depending on the type of project, there's varying amounts of travel. If you are working on a project that involves a new building, most of that work is usually done from the office. If it's a commissioning project or an existing building, there's travel to and from the site involved.

How Do You Become a Mechanical Engineer?

Education

A bachelor's degree in mechanical engineering is a necessity for entry-level jobs in mechanical engineering. Such degrees focus on math, life and physical science, and engineering and design courses. Some college programs offer a five- to six-year degree program that combines class work with an ongoing internship with a company to have hands-on experience with solving mechanical problems in the real world. Government agencies such as the National Aeronautics and Space Administration (NASA) and private companies such as Rockwell and Boeing have internship programs that work in concert with college programs.

Jessica Ewing is a senior majoring in mechanical engineering with an emphasis in environmental engineering at California State University–Northridge. In an interview on the website TryEngineering, she spoke about the challenges of such a major: "Being an engineering major is not easy. You do have to sacrifice a lot of time and energy for your class projects and your homework. However, with working in teams, you will find that you build friendships, and sometimes the work ends up not really feeling like work. . . . It helps me to study alone first, then with a team so I can get any questions answered."

A mechanical engineer works on an intelligent system lighting fixture that combines LED lights with software and other technology. The work of a mechanical engineer can include development of new products as well as maintenance and redesign of existing ones.

Certification and Licensing

Engineers who offer services to the public in all fifty states and the District of Columbia require licensure. Licensed mechanical engineers are designated as PEs. The PE license generally requires a degree from an engineering program accredited by ABET, four years of relevant work experience, and a state exam. College graduates can start the licensing process by taking the Fundamentals of Engineering exam right after graduation. Engineers who pass this exam commonly are called engineers in training or engineer interns. After gaining requisite work experience, engineers in training can take a second exam, called the Principles and Practice of Engineering exam, for full licensure as a PE. Several states require continuing education to renew the license every year.

Voluntary certification programs are offered through professional organizations such as the American Society of Mechanical Engineers. Such certification can enhance a job candidate's desirability.

Volunteer Work and Internships

Abundant volunteer opportunities exist for mechanical engineers. The Institution of Mechanical Engineers is just one organization that coordinates volunteer efforts for companies. One specific opportunity such organizations offer is a chance for volunteers to go into classrooms to help students build models, robots, or small machines and expose them to the possibilities of mechanical engineering. Internships are also plentiful for mechanical engineers. Many colleges offer internships as part of their degree program.

Skills and Personality

Mechanical engineers are problem solvers. When they encounter a mechanical or technical problem, they get great satisfaction from coming up with solutions. They must be great communicators because they must listen and interpret what is needed and be able to explain a solution to others—both in oral and written presentations. They must work well in a team. Lucht confirms this on the iSEEK website. He says:

> The thing I like most is the interaction with clients and problem solving. I really enjoy digging into an existing building and understanding the history, the problem, and the solution. There are so many ways an HVAC [heating, ventilation, and air-conditioning] system cannot perform, and only a few ways it can. I really enjoy troubleshooting and using the process of elimination to figure out what the problem is. It's so rewarding to do projects like that because a lot of times you're coming in when a chronic problem has become really bad. The building operations people just really want it solved. If you can be that person to come in [and] solve that problem, they are forever grateful. It is tremendously rewarding to come in and solve something that's been broken for a long time that no one else could fix. For example, a few years back we were working on an expansion project for a museum that had been dealing with a problem for 20 years. It was really creating an energy consumption issue for the building and frustrating their staff. We came

in, took some data on the air system, evaluated that, and proposed a fix that saved them energy, improved their occupant comfort, and solved a problem they'd been dealing with forever. That kind of thing makes this business enjoyable for me.

Employers

Mechanical engineering is the second largest of the engineering professions. According to the Bureau of Labor Statistics, mechanical engineers work mostly in engineering services, research and development, manufacturing industries, and the federal government. The breakdown looks like this: 21 percent are in jobs related to architectural, engineering, and related services; 6 percent are in research and development in physical, engineering, and life sciences; 5 percent are in the manufacture of navigational, electromedical, and control instrument manufacture; 5 percent are in aerospace; and 5 percent work for the federal government. Others work in machinery manufacturing, automotive parts manufacture, and testing laboratories.

Specific fields that require mechanical engineers are automotive; biomedical; heating, ventilation, and air conditioning (HVAC); nuclear facilities; robotics; and teaching. At the college level, teaching requires a master's degree or PhD in mechanical engineering. Government agencies that employ mechanical engineers include the US Navy, US Patent and Trademark Office, US International Trade Commission, US Army Corps of Engineers, US Department of Energy, and even the US Postal Service.

Working Conditions

Most mechanical engineers work full time, with some working as many as sixty hours or more per week. They normally work in office settings, though some travel may be necessary when equipment is installed off-site and requires installation, training of personnel, or ongoing troubleshooting or maintenance.

Earnings

Average earnings for mechanical engineers are from $52,030 to $121,530. The median annual wage of mechanical engineers is $82,000, according to Indeed. According to the Bureau of Labor statistics, median salaries for certain areas of the industry are: the federal government, averaging $91,940; research and development in the physical, engineering, and life sciences, $88,190; aerospace product and parts manufacturing, $83,870; navigational, measuring, electromedical, and control instruments manufacturing, $83,310; architectural, engineering, and related services, $82,210.

Opportunities for Advancement

Advancement opportunities for mechanical engineers depend on the size of the company they work for and whether they keep up with the latest software and computer developments to streamline their work. Some of the possibilities include management, sales and marketing, or starting their own company or consulting firm.

What Is the Future Outlook for Mechanical Engineers?

Employment of mechanical engineers is expected to grow 9 percent from 2010 to 2020, slower than the average for all occupations. As with many other engineering jobs, to stay competitive, mechanical engineers must keep abreast of the latest technologies. Mechanical engineers need training in the latest software tools, such as Advanced Visualization Process. This software allows engineers and designers to take a project from the conceptual phase directly to a finished product, eliminating the need for prototypes. Industries expected to need engineers in the future are in manufacturing, especially in the redesign and manufacture of engines to make them more fuel efficient. Hybrid electric cars and clean energy are just two examples of the ongoing need for innovation for mechanical engineers. Mechanical engineers will continue to be involved in developing machinery to replace human labor. The fields of alternative energy and nanotechnology may offer new directions for occupational growth.

Find Out More

American Design Drafting Association
105 E. Main St.
Newbern, TN 38059
phone: (731) 627-0802
fax: (731) 627-9321
e-mail: corporate@adda.org
website: www.adda.org

The American Design Drafting Association is an international non-profit professional membership and educational organization. The organization was conceived by a dedicated and enthusiastic group of oil and gas piping drafters who were involved in various phases of design drafting. This group consisted of highly specialized industry drafters, educational instructors, piping designers, and engineering personnel.

American Society of Heating, Refrigerating,
and Air-Conditioning Engineers (ASHRAE)
1791 Tullie Cir. NE
Atlanta, GA 30329
phone: (800) 527-4723 (US and Canada only)
fax: (404) 321-5478
website: www.ashrae.org

The ASHRAE is a building technology society that focuses on building systems, energy efficiency, indoor air quality, refrigeration, and sustainability within the industry. Through research, standards writing, publishing, and continuing education, the ASHRAE works to ensure the future of indoor heating and cooling.

American Society of Mechanical Engineers (ASME)
2 Park Ave.
New York, NY 10016
phone: (800) 843-2763 (US and Canada only)
e-mail: CustomerCare@asme.org
website: www.asme.org

The ASME is a not-for-profit membership organization that enables collaboration, knowledge sharing, career enrichment, and skills development across all engineering disciplines. It aims to help the global engineering community develop solutions to benefit lives and livelihoods.

Chemical Engineer

What Does a Chemical Engineer Do?

Chemical engineering is considered one of the four major engineering disciplines. The other three are electrical, mechanical, and civil. Chemical engineers have a broad education—rigorous training in chemistry as well as training in physics, mathematics, biology, and geology.

The chemical engineer's broad education translates into a large number of jobs he or she can do. At its essence, chemical engineering applies chemistry to make useful products and processes that have wide-ranging effects on the real world. Chemical engineers work on technical scientific endeavors such as splitting the atom or making plastics, rubber, medications, and synthetic blood, as well as on everyday products such as foods, cosmetics, and stain-resistant carpeting. Chemical engineers are also involved in streamlining processes to keep costs down on other products. For example, ammonia is used to make fertilizer; if ammonia can be made more efficiently and more cheaply, it can help keep costs down for fertilizer used by farmers in the developing world.

At a Glance:

Chemical Engineer

Minimum Educational Requirements
Bachelor's degree

Personal Qualities
Strong interest in chemistry, math, and physics; enjoy problem solving; good written and oral language skills; team player

Certification and Licensing
May be required for some jobs

Working Conditions
Indoors in an office or lab setting

Salary Range
About $56,520 to $139,670

Number of Jobs
As of 2013 about 32,190 in the United States

Future Job Outlook
Slower than average; growth rate of 6 percent from 2010 to 2020

Chemical engineers are found in other industries, too. They use their knowledge to improve methods of recycling plastics. Some chemical engineers are helping explore new ways to reduce dependence on fossil fuels, including through the use of hydrogen and various plant materials for new fuels. Chemical engineers develop processes and chemicals to make food products cheaper and safer and to increase yields. They work with computers to research and produce chemicals and chemical by-products. They also use computers to analyze complex data that come out of such research.

Chemical engineers usually specialize in one particular piece of the process, though some may be involved in all of them. Typically, there are five areas of specialty: research and development, design and construction, operations and production, environmental and waste management, and sales.

Chemical engineers who specialize in research and development work in a variety of industries to develop new products or revamp or redesign an existing product. They may work with a chemist or other type of scientist, depending on where they work. For example, a chemical engineer who works in a pharmaceutical company may be engaged in developing and testing a new drug as well as determining what form and what dose will be required. This may include conducting experiments that include the drug as well as developing a process to produce the drug. One job advertisement for such an engineer described the particular knowledge the engineer would need. It listed various aspects of the drug-making process, including "reaction, purification, distillation, crystallization, separation, and drying" as well as "milling, granulation, tablet compression, and coating." Once the formulation of the new product has passed tests that prove its effectiveness, its production is transferred to a pilot plant, where it is then subjected to further testing. At the pilot plant, which is a simplified version of a commercial plant, chemical engineers seek to further refine the processes of production, including reducing safety hazards, curtailing waste, streamlining production, and cutting costs. During this phase a new product may be abandoned for various reasons, including that the time and cost of making the new product outweighs the company's ability to sell it.

Once a product passes this stage, project managers take over the design and construction of plants and equipment to make it. Chemical engineers at this stage computerize the process so that production is consistent, waste is minimized, and efficiency is maximized. Field engineers will train people to use the machines and will assist in quality control. Not unlike project managers, chemical engineers in operations and production do similar tasks in an actual production plant after a product has passed from the pilot stage into full-blown production. In this capacity, chemical engineers oversee the plant, its employees, and all phases of production, including obtaining raw materials to develop the product and continuing to refine and streamline production procedures. Further refinement of processes could also be an area for a chemical engineer specializing in environmental and waste management. These engineers seek out the best ways to use raw materials, decrease waste, and, if the process results in pollution, reduce the impact of production on the environment.

Once the product reaches the marketplace, chemical engineers who specialize in technical sales are the ones on the front lines with the customer. They must not only know the product they are selling, but excel in people skills and oral communication to aid customers in the buying and use of the product. If the customer has complaints, this engineer is also in charge of answering to the customer and communicating back to the company about potential problems.

Thomas Niederkorn is a chemical engineer who works as a core technology leader in the food development department of Procter & Gamble. Niederkorn's job is typical of someone with a chemical engineering degree, though it is complicated to explain. In an interview on the website TryEngineering, he says of his job:

> You might consider the department I work for, the process expertise center for the company. We're the process experts in a number of what we call our "core processing technologies." These are fairly common chemical engineering unit operations—liquid mixing, heat transfer, heat exchanges. With each of these technologies, we have a group of people who support the company in that technology. And we have a number of different types of support. We do consulting on actual business projects with our customers. We call them customers, but these business areas are within the company. We do a lot of training and what we call technology transfer, which is

taking information that we've learned in one part of the company and reapplying it in other areas. We also do technology development, which is trying to maintain state-of-the-art in a particular technology area.

How Do You Become a Chemical Engineer?

Education

For some students interested in chemical engineering, the path may begin as early as junior high. At this young age some students take prerequisite math and science courses to prepare for higher-level courses in high school. Typically, a student should take four years of math and science courses, including physics, chemistry, trigonometry, and calculus, to prepare to enter college with a major in chemical engineering. Students pursuing a chemical engineering major should go to a school with an ABET program. Courses required in a chemical engineering program include chemistry, computing techniques, physics, and chemical reaction engineering as well as courses required of all engineering disciplines, such as thermodynamics, process design, and heat, mass, and momentum transfer. At some universities five-year programs are available in which a student can obtain both a bachelor's and master's degree in chemical engineering. Universities may offer programs that combine classroom study with work study, which allows students to apply internship or job credits to their degree while earning money to support themselves in college. Chemical engineer Chris Haslego, quoted on the website Cheresources.com, talks about the commitment required to become a chemical engineer:

> If you're considering studying Chemical Engineering, but you're a little timid because of the horror stories that you hear, you actually may want to think about it some more!
>
> I've actually heard someone say, "How hard can it be?" Really hard, but really rewarding too! True, the material involved is far from easy and some of the concepts take hours (and in some cases years!) to master, but isn't having this degree worth the effort?

I think that you'll find that it will be. I guess what I'm saying is, if you're serious about wanting to be a Chemical Engineer, go for it and don't be afraid to fail (as long as you've done your best). If you're not sure what you want to do, take some preliminary courses first and then ask some of the current students what they think so far and compare you're academic merit to theirs.

Certification and Licensing

Chemical engineers who become licensed carry the designation of PEs. To become licensed, chemical engineers must graduate from an ABET-accredited engineering program, pass both the Fundamentals of Engineering and the Professional Engineering exams, and have some relevant work experience. The PE exam can be taken after a student obtains his or her bachelor's degree. While getting work experience, engineers can take the second exam, Principles and Practice of Engineering. Haslego thinks it is especially important to take the exams: "I suggest taking the Fundamentals of Engineering Exam (FE Exam) shortly before or after graduation. Then after 4 or 5 years of industrial work, you can take the Professional Engineering Exam (PE Exam) and become a Certified Professional Engineer. Always a good idea to take these exams, remember, if you don't someone else will and they'll probably get your job!"

Volunteer Work and Internships

For both students and graduates of chemical engineering, volunteer work and internships abound. Many companies, both in the private and government sector, offer internships, and many organizations offer volunteer work throughout the world.

Skills and Personality

A strong interest in chemistry, math, and physics is mandatory to become a chemical engineer. The ability to think analytically, solve problems, and be creative is essential to be successful. Because projects often involve complex processes and problems that require teamwork and the preparation of reports, good interpersonal, oral, and written communication skills are also essential.

On the Job

Employers

Chemical engineers are some of the highest-paid engineers and have a variety of choices when it comes to employers. According to the Bureau of Labor Statistics, basic chemical manufacturing and scientific and developmental research are the largest areas of jobs for these engineers. They are employed in companies that deal with natural and environmental resource products, including oil, coal, and gas extraction. They also work for food, pharmaceutical, and agricultural companies. More cutting-edge fields include biotechnology and nanotechnology. There are more than thirty-two thousand engineers employed in the United States, and Texas, California, and Louisiana have the greatest number of engineering jobs. Niederkorn says that there are some advantages to taking a job with a large corporation such as Procter & Gamble:

> A lot of people are uncertain about whether they want to work for a large company. One thing I really like about working with a large company is the business impact that you can make. One of the very first projects I had out of school that I completed was worth millions of dollars to the company. So you go from a situation in school to work, where you're immediately given responsibility to work on very high-value projects. I really enjoy that; it motivates me a lot. It's kind of nice to come home at the end of the day and know that you had a $20 million impact on a project you just completed. The other thing that's becoming probably more and more common is globalization. Another aspect I like about my job with [Procter & Gamble] is that we also support the company globally outside North America, so we get to work on engineering projects around the world—designs that you are coming up with are being executed and implemented across the globe.

Working Conditions

Nearly all engineers work full time with regular overtime. They usually work indoors in a lab or desk setting, though some travel extensively to locations if their company works with other companies within or outside the United States.

Earnings

Chemical engineers are some of the highest-paid engineers. According to the American Institute of Chemical Engineers, the median salary was $120,000 in 2013—a 9 percent increase over the median reported in 2011. Unemployment has decreased in this field, and almost all full-time engineers receive retirement benefits. Median salaries range from $67,000 for chemical engineers with fewer than six years of experience to about $140,000 for those with more than thirty years in the workforce. The lowest 10 percent earned less than $56,520, and the top 10 percent earned more than $139,670.

Opportunities for Advancement

Many chemical engineers move on from hands-on work to managers, supervisors, and/or sales after the first five years of employment. They can also become lead engineers, supervising a particular product or research project.

What Is the Future Outlook for Chemical Engineers?

Employment of chemical engineers is expected to grow 6 percent from 2010 to 2020, slower than the average for all occupations. New emerging technologies such as nanotechnology, alternative energy, and biotechnology may increase the need for chemical engineers.

Find Out More

American Chemical Society (ACS)
1155 Sixteenth St. NW
Washington, DC 20036
phone: (800) 227-5558
e-mail: help@acs.org
website: www.ACS.org

The ACS is the world's largest scientific society and one of the world's leading sources of authoritative scientific information. A nonprofit organization chartered by Congress, the ACS is at the forefront of the evolving worldwide chemical enterprise and the premier professional home for chemists, chemical engineers, and related professions around the globe.

American Institute of Chemical Engineers (AIChE)
120 Wall St., 23rd Floor
New York, NY 10005
phone: (800) 242-4363
website: www.AIChE.org

The AIChE is the world's leading organization for chemical engineering professionals, with more than forty-five thousand members from more than ninety countries. The AIChE offers resources such as ongoing education classes and publications in all fields of chemical engineering, including emerging areas such as nanobiotechnology.

International Society of Pharmaceutical Engineers (ISPE)
600 N. Westshore Blvd., Suite 900
Tampa, FL 33609
phone: (813) 960-2105
e-mail: ASK@ispe.org
website: http://ISPE.org

The ISPE works to keep industry professionals informed of the latest technological and regulatory trends that are occurring in the marketplace. The ISPE is committed to the advancement of the educational and technical efficiency of its members through forums for the exchange of ideas and practical experience.

National Organization for the Professional Advancement of Black Chemists and Chemical Engineers (NOBCChE)
PO Box 77040
Washington, DC 20013
phone: (800) 776-1419
website: www.nobcche.org

The primary purpose of NOBCChE is to initiate and support local, regional, national, and global programs that assist people of color in fully realizing their potential in academic, professional, and entrepreneurial pursuits in chemistry, chemical engineering, and related fields. The organization promotes careers in science and technology as an achievable goal for elementary, middle, and high school students.

Aerospace Engineer

What Does an Aerospace Engineer Do?

The broadest possible definition of an aerospace engineer is someone who researches, designs, develops, tests, manufactures, and maintains aerospace vehicles and systems such as commercial and military aircraft, missiles, spacecraft, and related aerospace equipment. The field of aerospace engineering entails several areas of study, some of which can apply to other engineering fields—but all are essential for a career in this field. They include thermodynamics, fluid mechanics, propulsion, structures, celestial mechanics, acoustics, and guidance and control. As applied to aerospace engineering, thermodynamics involves questions such as the heat stress on an airplane or airship during reentry; fluid mechanics are essential in the study of aerodynamics, including the size and shape of an air-transport vehicle; propulsion is essential to the design and movement of any vehicle, in this case those moving within and outside the atmosphere; the study of structures applies to the ability of the vehicle to maintain external shape and the weight load; celestial mechanics is an understanding of how particles move in space. For an aerospace engineer, celestial mechanics may involve orbits and trajectory, acoustics both inside and outside a vehicle, the study of sonic booms, guidance and control systems for takeoffs and landings, and maintaining speed and control of a vehicle. All of these areas are significantly different in space than on land. Engineers typically specialize in either aeronautics (aircraft), or astronautics (spacecraft).

Aerospace engineers often specialize in a particular area based on their chosen field of study. Those who specialize in aerodynamics work with software and designers to study the design of aircraft and how they fly. They use a wind tunnel to study the effects of air flowing over the vehicle to make sure it has maximum efficiency in fuel use and movement. Aerospace engineers who specialize in structure analyze stress on the vehicle during takeoff, landing, and reentry. They consider how much the structure can carry while under duress, how much fuel is required, and the safety and durability of the structure. Design engineers are responsible for the design of new aircraft or spacecraft. They must have a broad understanding of all of the areas of study listed above. They must have extensive knowledge of computers, not only to design new products but to conduct computerized tests to understand the viability of the design. Some aerospace engineers specialize in testing models and prototypes once a design is accepted in its initial stages. They make modifications to the aircraft design as well as test its performance. Materials engineers choose the materials that are used in building aircraft and spacecraft. For instance, materials engineers took part in choosing the heat shield tiles that were used on the US space shuttles. Various considerations went into this selection. Among these were the ability of the tiles to endure the stress and heat of leaving and reentering the atmosphere, withstand the temperatures of space, and keep the astronauts safe throughout take-offs, orbit, and landings. Materials engineers must also advise on how to manufacture the materials and oversee the processes that are required. They are also in charge of the cost and schedule of the materials. They also must work in concert with other engineers on the project when something goes wrong or when a material is underperforming.

Sales and marketing aerospace engineers are the liaison between the customer and the company. They establish an ongoing relationship with the client after they sell a product, making sure it is what the customer wants and bringing back questions as well as complaints and needs for adjustment that the client makes.

How Do You Become an Aerospace Engineer?

Education

The time to start planning for a career in this field is junior high school. This is because a student should take college-track courses in high school to be able to enter an engineering program. Anyone who is interested in an aerospace career must do well in higher-level math and science classes, including trigonometry, calculus, physics, and chemistry. All of these courses provide essential preparation for a career in the aerospace field. Students should make sure to choose a college that has an accredited program accepted by ABET. A bachelor's degree in engineering with a focus on general engineering principles, propulsion, stability and control, structures, mechanics, and aerodynamics is important. Some schools offer five-year programs in which the student can obtain both a bachelor's and master's degree upon completion. Some colleges offer work-study programs in which students can gain academic credit while working at an internship or job with an aerospace-related private company or government agency such as NASA.

Certification and Licensing

Although voluntary, most states require engineers to be licensed. Some aerospace engineers may choose to seek one of two levels of licensure. In addition to their degree, PEs must have four years of work experience and pass a written exam, Principles and Practice of Engineering. Some students pursue another route to the same goal by taking and passing the Fundamentals of Engineering exam immediately after graduation. Those graduates are then designated as engineers in training or engineer interns. After acquiring work experience, they can take the final exam and gain a full PE certification.

John Connolly, an engineer at the Johnson Space Center in Houston, believes ongoing education in this field is essential. He explains his thinking on a website for the state of Texas, Labor Market and Career Information: "I'm a certified engineer, and I do what I need to get re-certified every year. And I read a lot! At least one magazine daily. I read science fiction, Einstein's theory of relativity, anything with the word 'space' in it. I also go on the Internet and read NASAWATCH. I've been helping to write a textbook: Human Space Mission and Design, so I've done a lot of reading for that, too."

Volunteer Work and Internships

There are many opportunities for volunteer work and internships for high school and college students. Numerous summer camps around the country offer programs that build experimental aircraft and rockets. Working with a high school teacher to design and build a model aircraft is another possibility. In college engineering students often participate in co-ops to build and experiment with projects. Many colleges work in concert with the American Institute of Aeronautics and Astronautics to offer student chapters on campus. The institute offers many benefits, including competitions, scholarships, and opportunities to have professionals in the field speak on campus. In addition, NASA offers many internship opportunities for those pursuing this field. The organization also offers competitions and opportunities for students to test prototypes in environments simulating space.

Skills and Personality

Along with a strong interest in science and math, those pursuing an aerospace engineering career need to be questioners, asking why something does what it does. They also must be patient yet determined to persevere in the face of obstacles, excellent problem solvers, and detail oriented. They must also have excellent oral and written communication skills. Finally, they must be good team players and enjoy working with others to solve problems.

Aerospace engineer Julie A. Pollitt, interviewed on the website TryEngineering, knew as a child that she wanted to work in aerospace engineering. She was influenced by her grandfather, who urged her to watch all of the televised NASA space missions. She says:

> When I was about 16, when I was in high school, I made the firm decision that I was going to work for NASA no matter what. So I started talking with college recruiters and different companies and the military and asked a lot of them what types of degrees or what NASA would look for. I didn't come prepared with a lot of money so I was assuming that I was going to Air Force ROTC. And I was actually four years in a wheelchair. I was injured when I was in high school. So they had said that engineering, aerospace engineering, would be a

good field to go into to work for NASA. And I was going to go Air Force ROTC, become an aerospace engineer and then go on to work for NASA. . . . And then I just headed down that path. I headed for a college for engineering. I grew up in Connecticut, so I went to University of Connecticut, got a Bachelor's . . . and headed on and dropped everything and left for California. Came out to NASA Ames Research Center. Knocked on their door and asked them for a job. And fortunately, within a day I was hired.

On the Job

Employers

Aerospace engineers held about 80,420 jobs in 2013. They are employed by companies that design or build aircraft, missiles, systems for national defense, or spacecraft. According to the Bureau of Labor Statistics for 2012, the vast majority of aerospace engineers, 35 percent, were employed in aerospace product and parts manufacturing. Fifteen percent were employed in architectural, engineering, and related services; 14 percent in scientific research and development; 13 percent by the federal government; and 8 percent in navigational, measuring, electromedical, and control instrument manufacturing. Top states that employ aerospace engineers include California, Washington, and Texas. Some of the top companies that employ aerospace engineers include BAE Systems, Lockheed Martin, General Dynamics, Boeing, Northrop Grumman, the US Department of Defense, and NASA.

Working Conditions

With ever more sophisticated computer software becoming an important part of their job, aerospace engineers spend less time in the field and more time indoors in a lab or office setting. However, those who work in field testing or flight testing may be out in the field. A few who work on space projects such as the *International Space Station* or the shuttle could even find themselves working in space.

Earnings

According to Indeed, in 2013 the salary range for aerospace engineers was $58,000 to $128,000, which is a 36 percent higher range than average job postings nationwide. Jobs that pay in the lower range are aerospace production engineer, manufacturing engineer, and airframe design engineer. The highest-paid jobs in this field include senior aerospace systems engineer, cement mechanical engineer, and stress engineer.

Opportunities for Advancement

As with all engineering careers, more experienced aerospace engineers usually work on more complex projects and demand higher pay. After five to six years on the job, they are often offered management opportunities or lead engineer opportunities. A chief engineer in charge of a particular project and those who work on it usually demands the highest pay.

What Is the Future Outlook for Aerospace Engineers?

According to the Bureau of Labor Statistics, employment of aerospace engineers is expected to grow 4.9 percent from 2010 to 2020, slower than the average for all occupations. Aerospace engineers who work on projects that are related to national defense and require security clearances are guaranteed to continue holding jobs in the United States. Other areas under development that will help employ aerospace engineers are projects to design aircraft that are less noisy and more fuel efficient. While the US government has been curbing its hiring in the space industry, private companies have taken over somewhat in that regard, including developing aircraft to take private citizens into space.

The Bureau of Labor Statistics predicts that aerospace engineers who are experienced at collaborative engineering tools and processes and who know about modeling, simulation, and robotics will continue to have good job prospects. They also predict good opportunities for engineers trained in Computational Fluid Dynamics software, which enables companies to test designs in a digital environment and thereby lower testing costs.

Find Out More

Aerospace Industries Association (AIA)
1000 Wilson Blvd., Suite 1700
Arlington, VA 22209
phone: (703) 358-1000
website: http://aia-aerospace.org

The AIA represents the nation's leading manufacturers and suppliers of civil, military, and business aircraft, helicopters, unmanned aircraft systems, space systems, aircraft engines, missiles, materiel and related components, equipment, services, and information technology.

American Astronomical Society (AAS)
2000 Florida Ave. NW, Suite 300
Washington, DC 20009
phone: (202) 328-2010
e-mail: aas@aas.org
website: http://aas.org

The mission of the AAS is to enhance and share humanity's scientific understanding of the universe. Through its publications, the society disseminates and archives the results of astronomical research. The AAS trains, mentors, and supports the next generation of astronomers. It also supports and promotes increased participation of historically underrepresented groups in astronomy.

National Aeronautics and Space Administration (NASA)
Public Communications Office
Suite 2R40
Washington, DC 20546
phone: (202) 358-0001
fax: (202) 358-4338
website: www.NASA.gov

NASA works to make aircraft more environmentally friendly and sustainable; focuses on *International Space Station* operations and development of commercial spaceflight capabilities; explores the Earth, solar system, and universe beyond; and develops, innovates, demonstrates, and infuses revolutionary technologies. It sponsors many educational opportunities for students of all ages and is an employer of many aerospace engineers.

Environmental Engineer

What Does an Environmental Engineer Do?

Environmental engineering is an offshoot of civil engineering and incorporates an understanding of biology, soil science, chemistry, and engineering to solve environmental problems. Environmental engineers work in areas of waste disposal, public health, and pollution control. They may also work to solve global issues related to clean water, climate change, and sustainability issues. They are involved in many different areas and work with a wide variety of people and organizations, including both domestic and international private companies, federal and state governments, and private citizens. Environmental engineers must use computer models to assess the environmental impacts of large projects such as new sewer and waste treatment plants. They do this to prevent environmental problems and to monitor and clean up existing problems. They must continu-

---

At a Glance:

Environmental Engineer

Minimum Educational Requirements
Bachelor's degree

Personal Qualities
Technical/scientific interests; strong communication skills; problem solver; tolerates outdoor work in sometimes hazardous health conditions

Certification and Licensing
Voluntary; PE license encouraged

Working Conditions
Indoors; outdoors at specific sites

Salary Range
About $48,980 to $119,060

Number of Jobs
As of 2012 about 51,000 in the United States

Future Job Outlook
Better than average; growth rate of 22 percent from 2010 to 2020

ally upgrade their skills and knowledge to match new developments in engineering and environmental science.

The skills and talents of environmental engineers are applied to many different areas. These include:

- Hazardous waste management: Environmental engineers are called in whenever air, water, or soil is contaminated. They investigate such contamination by designing studies to understand the cause of the problem, identify solutions, and work with municipal and/or industrial wastewater plants to contain and remedy the problem. Environmental engineers who work for the government are involved in the prevention of spills. To ensure safe disposal, they monitor and enforce regulations during the building of treatment plants and industrial plants that generate waste. When spills occur, environmental engineers conduct water-quality assessments of lakes, rivers, groundwater, and aquifers. In some instances they might even be called to offer testimony of their findings in a court of law.

- Environmental engineers may be involved in identifying and solving environmental problems that occur on a global scale. They study problems and work to find solutions to acid rain, global warming, ozone depletion, and automobile and industrial air pollution. They work with other engineers as well as lawyers, businesses, governments, and urban planners to solve these problems.

- Environmental engineers may be heavily involved in the planning and design of water treatment plants. Their duties include conducting environmental site assessments to determine the impact a future plant will have on the environment. They advise about all things having to do with water, including minimizing water use, suggesting methods of water treatment, and offering proposals on safe disposal of waste in water and on land.

- Environmental engineers also work with air-quality assessment. They may conduct air-quality assessments and advise industrial clients on developing air-pollution control systems to minimize pollutants.

- When a company or government wants to build a land use project that might affect the environment—for example, gravel pits, pipelines, or a new airport—environmental engineers assess the environmental impact of such a project. They make recommendations on how to protect the surrounding land and water during the construction process and after the project is built. This is especially important when a project is planned near sensitive habitat such as wetlands or a nesting area for endangered birds. Environmental engineers also assist companies in acquiring permits to be in compliance with government rules and regulations.

An environmental engineer interviewed on Job Shadow described his job in a particularly interesting way:

> You could probably boil everything that I do down to the main concept that we want rivers to transport dirt correctly. Now that sounds pretty boring but it entails a river depositing too much sediment or eroding away too much sediment from the banks so what we do is we take the stream systems in urban or in rural settings and we rebuild them to reflect what they would have been had they been left natural. . . . We do all of the site analysis, the initial data collection. We do a lot of surveying with laser survey gear or aerial survey gear if we get flown. We do the request for proposals. We do the scope of work, all the paperwork associated with getting the project, then once we get the initial data we do the design. We do the contracting too and we use a lot of computer system design software. After the design is done we move into the construction that we oversee. And then afterwards, there's usually some period of monitoring involved where we say OK how has the habitat improved or not improved since we did this restoration so we can learn a little bit more.

How Do You Become an Environmental Engineer?

Education

Environmental engineers must have a bachelor's degree in environmental engineering or a related field such as civil, chemical, or mechanical engineering. Employers also value practical experience.

Therefore, cooperative engineering programs, in which college credit is awarded for structured job experience, are valuable as well.

High school students interested in studying environmental engineering in college should take chemistry, biology, physics, and mathematics, including algebra, trigonometry, and calculus. Students should choose a college with an engineering program accredited by ABET. A degree from an ABET-accredited program is usually necessary to become a licensed PE.

There are many educational paths to becoming an environmental engineer, and some colleges and universities do not offer a specific degree in the discipline. Some students study civil, mechanical, or chemical engineering and still go on to become an environmental engineer. Coursework includes traditional engineering courses such as fluid mechanics, higher mathematics and science courses, as well as computational modeling, organic chemistry, sanitary engineering, ecosystems, and aquatic chemistry. Many experts recommend that environmental engineers also obtain a PhD in environmental engineering to increase their knowledge and/or gain a specialty in a particular environmental field.

Certification and Licensing

Environmental engineers who become licensed carry the designation of PEs. To become licensed, environmental engineers must graduate from an ABET-accredited engineering program, pass both the Fundamentals of Engineering and the Professional Engineering exams, and have some relevant work experience. The PE exam can be taken after a student obtains his or her bachelor's degree. While getting work experience, engineers can take the second exam, Principles and Practice of Engineering. After obtaining the PE license, environmental engineers can become board certified from the American Academy of Environmental Engineers and Scientists. This certification shows that an environmental engineer has expertise in a particular area. Several states require continuing education for engineers to keep their license.

Volunteer Work and Internships

Once a student enters college, there are many opportunities to volunteer and to obtain paid and volunteer internships in environmental engineering. Nonprofit environmental groups frequently use students on projects, and many companies, including the Environmental Protection Agency, offer internships to students still in school.

Skills and Personality

Environmental engineers need to enjoy science and technology, working with mechanical devices, and lifelong learning, since they need to continually update their skill set. They often work and make decisions independently, and most people in this field are committed to improving the environment. They must also enjoy working in a team with many different types of people, some with a technical background, and laypeople. They also need to think logically and enjoy solving problems, and they should not mind working outdoors and sometimes dealing with hazardous pollutants. They must enjoy analyzing "the big picture" from as many angles as possible because they must examine problems that have an impact in different areas. As with all engineers, environmental engineers must be strong written and oral communicators, but the need is very important in this career since they are likely to work with many different people who have many different interests—such as business owners, government officials, lawyers, and private citizens. In addition, because they must often analyze documents that may be unfamiliar to them, they must have good reading comprehension skills.

An environmental engineer interviewed on Job Shadow says that people are under the mistaken impression that the job is "just strictly math, science, and formulas and is very boring and you're always at a computer with a bunch of nerds. But a lot of what we do is outdoors. A lot of it is data collection. A lot of it is site visits. It's not just the applying of the formulas. There's a lot of creativity. To design a stream, make it flow wherever you want it is very fun and it's usually with a lot of outdoorsy and outgoing people."

On the Job

Employers

About fifty-one thousand environmental engineers work in the United States. They work in various industries, including manufacturing; federal, state, and local governments; and engineering consulting companies. They can also work for chemical, oil, nuclear, and paper-making companies as well as at universities.

Working Conditions

The immense range of environmental engineers means that their work environment also varies greatly. A typical day may include such wide-ranging activities as working all day at a computer with models and simulations or visiting a public work site to assess compliance. They may also cover themselves in protective gear to evaluate a potential or existing hazardous spill. They can participate in a public hearing on a new project to testify about its impact on civilians. Sometimes environmental engineers are asked to testify in court in cases involving companies being prosecuted for criminal environmental negligence. Though environmental engineers regularly work in an office, some may have to travel for extended periods if they are working on the site of a hazardous spill.

For example, environmental engineers are involved in monitoring and assessing the international impact on water and soil from the nuclear accident that occurred in 2011 in Fukushima, Japan. They are continuing to assess the impact on Japan and other nations. They are also working with many other types of engineers to design methods for safely removing contaminated water and minimizing the damage in Japanese and international waters.

Earnings

According to Indeed, the median salary for an environmental engineer was $84,000 in 2013. According to the Bureau of Labor Statistics, in 2012 the lowest 10 percent earned less than $48,980, and the top 10 percent earned more than $119,060. In categories, environmental engineers were paid a median of $100,270 in federal government jobs; $78,450 in architectural, engineering, and related services jobs; $75,280 in local government jobs; $74,940 in management, scientific, and technical consulting service jobs; and $69,050 in state government jobs. Most environmental engineers work full time, and travel may be required.

Opportunities for Advancement

As for many engineering careers, environmental engineers go into management, supervision, and/or sales after the first five years of employment. They can also become lead engineers, supervising a particular product or research project.

What Is the Future Outlook for Environmental Engineers?

The outlook for the period from 2010 to 2020 is better than the industry average for engineers and is expected to grow by 22 percent. For many private industries and governments, the goal is to prevent environmental problems before they happen, and this has meant new opportunities for environmental engineers. In addition, the government continues to deal with cleaning up contaminated areas, and environmental engineers remain on the forefront of these efforts. On the other hand, many government positions for environmental engineers are subject to government cutbacks, which may decrease opportunities in the field.

Find Out More

American Academy of Environmental
Engineers and Scientists (AAEES)
147 Old Solomons Island Rd., Suite 303
Annapolis, MD 21401
phone: (410) 266-3311
fax: (410) 266-7653
website: http://aaees.org

The AAEES is a group of environmental engineers and environmental scientists who have imposed self-testing and review for entry qualification. Each Board Certified Environmental Engineer, Board Certified Environmental Engineering Member, and Board Certified Environmental Scientist has not only the standard prerequisites for specialty certification but also has passed written and oral examinations and reviews by an admission panel of the academy.

Environmental Protection Agency (EPA)
1200 Pennsylvania Ave. NW
Washington, DC 20460
phone: (202) 272-0167
website: www.epa.gov

The EPA is the primary government environmental organization in the United States and a major employer of environmental professionals. The EPA is given the mission of assuring that all Americans are protected from significant risks to human health and the environment where they live, learn, and work. It lists internships, grant possibilities, and jobs on its website.

National Association of Environmental Professionals (NAEP)
PO Box 460
Collingswood, NJ 08108
phone: (856) 283-7816
fax: (856) 210-1619
e-mail: naep@bowermanagementservices.com
website: www.naep.org

The NAEP is dedicated to developing the highest standards of ethics and proficiency in the environmental professions. Its members are public- and private-sector professionals who promote excellence in decision making in light of the environmental, social, and economic impacts of those decisions. It seeks to be a primary source of unbiased information on environmental practices, support the advancement of the environmental professions, and encourage better decision making.

Water Environment Federation (WEF)
601 Wythe St.
Alexandria, VA 22314
phone: (800) 666-0206
e-mail: csc@wef.org
website: www.wef.org

The WEF is a not-for-profit international technical and educational organization. Its global network of members provides water-quality professionals around the world with the latest in water-quality education, training, and business opportunities. The federation's diverse membership includes scientists, engineers, regulators, academics, utility managers, plant operators, and other professionals. The WEF uses this collective knowledge to further a shared goal of improving water quality around the world.

Interview with an Electrical Engineer

R ick Fulton is an electrical engineer for BAE Systems, an international company that works primarily with the military. He has worked as an electrical engineer for more than thirty years. He spoke with the author about his career.

Q: Why did you become an electrical engineer?

A: I didn't start out wanting to be an engineer. When I first went to college, I wanted to be an art major. Once I started taking art classes, I realized that for one thing, I didn't have the talent to become an artist and secondly it wasn't going to pay well. I started looking at different majors and studying the college's statistics on graduates—which majors made the most money, as well as which majors had high job placement rates. Hands down, engineering was near the top, so I decided to become an engineer.

Q: Can you describe your typical workday?

A: It isn't what I thought it was going to be like when I first graduated. I thought I was going to be designing new stuff every day. What I quickly learned is that for every small thing that is designed, there is a lot of documentation that needs to be done. In order to make a design become a salable product, it has to go through many steps, including building usable models, testing those models, reassembling them, and many other steps. Analysis is the largest part of my day, every day. It's important to test your component under many different conditions and stressors.

Q: What do you like most and least about your job?

A: I love the design phase the most. I love the research—you learn a lot about something new, something you've never delved into before. It's fun! It reminds me of playing with Tinkertoys when I was a kid—testing different scenarios, trying to break the thing you are building. I once had to design a circuit to drive a speaker, and to test it I turned it up as loud as it would go and left it in my desk drawer overnight. When I got in the next morning, it was still blaring away—that's satisfying!

My least favorite part of the job is what I mentioned above—the documentation. But the absolute worst thing is that you don't design in a vacuum—what you make has to meet management's cost and production expectations. You have to compromise, you can't make something the way you think is the best way or the right way. Management tells you to stop building—stop tinkering—and start building! An engineer wants to make sure that something will fail one time in fifty thousand uses, while management is happy with a one in five thousand failure rate.

Q: What personal qualities do you find most valuable for this type of work?

A: I discourage people from becoming an engineer if they don't absolutely love math and science. You really do have to use them every day. You also have to be willing to work on something someone else designed and not get frustrated that it's "not your problem." You often work long hours and have a sense of responsibility for your design—making sure that it will work. You have to be willing to stay with a problem and try different things and not get discouraged when you hit dead ends.

Q: What advice do you have for students who might be interested in this career?

A: You have to be engineering-minded—in other words, you have to constantly wonder about how something works. The best engineers are interested in electricity, or mechanics, or building things—from a very young age. The difference between an electrical engineer and an electrician, for example, is discipline. The study of engineering is hard—you have to learn a lot of mathematics, a lot of science that you may never need. But you stick with it because that is part of the discipline. One of my professors used to say that the reason you have to learn so much math, for example, is to prove that you are capable of learning it—you must be capable of learning new material and be able to go in depth with the topic—whenever it presents itself, even if you've never encountered it before. The fact that you learned calculus means that you are capable of learning other complex subjects.

Other Jobs in Engineering

Actuary
Astronomer
Automotive engineer
Aviation inspector
Aviation mechanic
Biochemist
Biophysicist
Budget analyst
Building site manager
Chemist and materials scientist
Computer network support
   specialist
Computer programmer
Computer systems analyst
Data administrator
Drafter
Electrical and electronics
installer
Electrician
Electromechanical technician
Environmental compliance
   inspector
Environmental engineering
   technician

Environmental scientist
Fish and game warden
Hydrologist
Insurance claims inspector
Machinist
Marine biologist
Mathematician
Mechanical drafter
Medical appliance technician
Mining/geological engineer
Natural science manager
Nuclear engineer
Orthotist/prosthetist
Petroleum engineer
Physicist
Pilot
Satellite systems engineer
Science teacher
Software developer
Statistician
Surveyor
Traffic technician
Web designer/developer
Welder

Editor's Note: The online *Occupational Outlook Handbook* of the US Department of Labor's Bureau of Labor Statistics is an excellent source of information on jobs in hundreds of career fields including many of those listed here. The *Occupational Outlook Handbook* may be accessed online at www.bls.gov/ooh/.

Index

About the Author

Bonnie Szumski has been an editor and author of nonfiction books for more than twenty-five years.